NO NONSENSE COOKING GUIDE

MICROWAVE MAIN COURSES

QUICK & EASY

NO NONSENSE COOKING GUIDE

MICROWAVE MAIN COURSES

QUICK & EASY

IRENA CHALMERS

LONGMEADOW PRESS

The recipes contained in this book have been tested and tried. However, results may vary depending on the conditions in your kitchen.

STAFF FOR NO NONSENSE COOKING GUIDES

EDITORIAL DIRECTION: Jean Atcheson

MANAGING EDITOR: Mary Goodbody

COVER DESIGN: Karen Skelton

ART DIRECTION & DESIGN: Helene Berinsky

RECIPE DEVELOPMENT: Marilyn Schanze, Cynthia Salvino
AMERICAN COOKING INSTITUTE, ST. JOSEPH, MICHIGAN

ASSISTANT EDITORS: Mary Dauman, Dorothy Atcheson

PROJECT MANAGER: Nancy Kipper

COVER PHOTOGRAPH: Gerald Zanetti

TYPESETTING: ComCom, Allentown, Pennsylvania

PRODUCTION SERVICES: William S. Konecky Associates, New York

CONTENTS

ACKNOWLEDGMENTS

Grateful acknowledgment is made to the following for permission to reproduce or adapt original recipes:

Bounty Microwave Paper Towels, Procter and Gamble; Campbell Soup Company; Corning Glass Works; Lamb Education Center; Ms. Thelma Pressman; Reynolds Metal Company

MICROWAVE MAIN COURSES

Meals in minutes. This is what we expect the microwave to make for us: to liberate us from long hours laboring over a hot stove and to cook the foods we like to eat with no loss of flavor or goodness. And it can. The microwave can perform nearly all the cooking functions of a conventional oven and stove top *combined*—frequently in half the time (or less) and with *very* satisfying results.

Using a microwave, it is perfectly possible to cook chicken and fish in minutes, to prepare a casserole in half an hour, and to make rich vegetable soup in less than an hour. But wondrous as these cooking times are, the microwave is far more than a time saver. It is a gentle and reliable cooking system that, with practice, becomes an indispensable kitchen tool.

When it comes to the heart of the meal, the main course, the microwave is in its element. Its efficiency lets you prepare perfectly cooked, moist, tender food in a very short time. This is an obvious advantage on weeknights, especially. After-work frenzy subsides when the *whole* meal, including the salad, bread and

7

perhaps a second vegetable, appears on the table in under an hour. It is equally useful on more leisurely weekends, giving you time to bake a loaf of bread or prepare a spectacular dessert without worrying about finding the hours you once needed to prepare the main course.

And, of course, on those hot, humid days when the thought of turning on the conventional oven seems nonsensical, yet a main course *has* to be cooked—the microwave can be a savior, cooking it quietly and quickly without adding to the heat in your kitchen.

Microwave main courses range from homey chowders and gumbos, simple fish fillets and chicken stir-fries to more sophisticated fare such as stuffed sole and a rare beef roast. Some of the ideas found on these pages ask for no more than to be served with a crisp green salad and a glass of chilled white wine. Others deserve more elaborate vegetable side dishes and perhaps even a first course to whet the appetite, and certainly a sumptuous dessert to round out the full-course meal. In such cases, it is quite possible to prepare nearly the entire menu in the microwave—but it is by no means essential.

Think of the microwave as a kitchen tool that is there to help you, not to render the rest of the kitchen equipment obsolete. You might want to cook the vegetable in the microwave simply because when microwaved, vegetables retain all their moisture, color, flavor and texture. On the other hand, you might choose to cook a rice pilaf or risotto very slowly on the conventional stove, reserving the microwave for the main course and the vegetable.

However you choose to use the microwave, remember that it is a cooking method, not a space-age phenomenon that magically "zaps" food into a state of doneness with the push of a button. The size, shape and temperature of the food make a difference in how it will react to the microwaves and how quickly and well it will cook. Generally speaking, small, evenly sized pieces of food at room temperature cook faster than large, dense, irregularly shaped food that is cold. Many recipes require a "standing" time, in which the internal temperature of the food continues to cook it for a few minutes after it has been removed from the microwave. Always check for doneness by tasting, piercing the food with a fork or knife, or looking for other obvious signs.

All this bodes particularly well for main course foods such as fish, chicken, ground beef, thinly sliced veal, casseroles and stews. These—and many other dishes too—really can be prepared in the microwave "in minutes" and will arrive at the table piping hot, bursting with true flavor and with a most pleasing texture. Could you ask for more?

USING YOUR MICROWAVE

MICROWAVE POWER AND TIMING

Most microwaves run on 600 to 700 watts, although some of the smaller models are less powerful. The recipes in this book have been developed for microwaves within this range but if yours is less than 600 watts, you will need to extend slightly the cooking times given in recipes.

Microwave cooking is not an exact science, so you cannot depend on time alone to determine when the food is cooked. Open the oven door during cooking to check the food for doneness and adjust times and power settings accordingly, just as you would in a conventional oven.

Remember: The amount of power can also be affected by various factors, such as use of other electrical equipment on the same circuit or even utility company procedures.

The temperature, size and shape of the food will affect the timing, too. Food at room temperature cooks more quickly than food just taken from the refrigerator.

POWER SETTINGS

Most of today's microwave ovens offer variable power settings ranging from High (100 percent power) to Low (10 percent). The higher settings are most often used for cooking or reheating, while the low settings are designed for simmering, defrosting or keeping food warm. Throughout this book, we have indicated the power percentage necessary for every recipe.

EQUIPMENT

You do not need any special utensils for basic microwave cooking, although as you become more adventurous you may want to invest in some of the equipment specially designed for the microwave, such as browning dishes or racks.

You cannot use metal containers, most aluminum foil, or even plates with a metallic trim because microwaves cannot pass through metal. If you put metal in the microwave, the waves will bounce off the metal and "arc," which means they will spark and sizzle. In some modern ovens, however, lightweight aluminum foil may be used for shielding parts of the food that might otherwise overcook.

Heatproof glass plates and dishes are ideal, as are most ceramics, porcelain or pottery. Test any utensil you are unsure about before using it in the microwave.

TESTING FOR "MICROWAVABILITY"

Put the utensil in the oven along with a 1-cup glass measure filled with tap water. Microwave on High (100 percent power) for 1 minute. If the dish remains cool while the water in the measure becomes hot, the utensil is safe to use, or "microwavable." If the dish becomes hot, it is absorbing microwave energy and should not be used. (During cooking, the transfer of heat from food *can* make microwavable dishes hot, so be sure to have potholders handy.)

MICROWAVE COOKING TECHNIQUES

Small, uniformly shaped pieces or amounts of food will cook more quickly than large. Shield the thinner parts of unevenly shaped foods to prevent overcooking.

Stir or rearrange food once or twice during the cooking process to help it cook more evenly. Rotating foods in the oven will achieve the same result.

Remember: Standing time is often part of cooking. Some foods will not seem completely cooked when removed from the microwave but the standing time will complete the process.

Use paper towels and plates, transparent wrap and wax paper in the microwave according to the recipe instructions. Dry plain white paper towels prevent spattering and absorb moisture. Wax paper makes a loose cover to hold in heat.

When a tight cover is needed to hold in steam and tenderize and cook food more evenly, use a casserole lid or transparent wrap rolled back slightly at one edge to allow for venting. Be careful of escaping steam as you remove a cover.

CHAPTER 1

MAIN COURSE SOUPS

On those evenings when you feel tugged in a hundred different directions—there is a meeting you must attend, one child is racing out the door while another is hanging around the kitchen waiting for something to eat—the perfect solution to supper is soup. A hearty, warming, soul-pleasing soup served with a loaf of bread or some warm rolls and a tossed green salad is a good, wholesome and satisfying meal.

With a microwave, soups are easy and fast to make. In minutes you can have a tureen full of steaming soup that your family will happily devour. Canned, frozen and packaged soups, no doubt already in your cupboard, speed up and simplify soup preparation. With a little planning, you can make soup from scratch during the weekend or on a weekday evening, when you have some extra time, and freeze it. Thawing and reheating it is no problem with a microwave. And leftover soup, stored in the refrigerator for several days, can easily be heated by the individual bowlful in the microwave— about 2 minutes on High (100 percent).

French Onion Soup

Serves 4

With its crusty topping of bread and melted cheese, this soup was always served to workers at Les Halles, the vast old central market of Paris. It kept them going through the long, dark hours before dawn and it is a perfect dish to keep anyone going during a chilly winter's day. Melting the cheese on top to soft, stringy deliciousness is easy in a microwave.

3 tablespoons (1½ ounces) butter
2 cups sliced onions
2 14½-ounce cans beef broth
3 beef bouillon cubes
4 slices melba toast
4 tablespoons freshly grated parmesan cheese

Put the butter in a 2-quart microwavable casserole. Microwave on High (100 percent) for 30 seconds until the butter is melted.

Add the onions to the casserole and stir to coat them with the melted butter. Cover and microwave on High (100 percent) for 5 to 6 minutes until the onions are softened. Add the beef broth and the bouillon cubes. Cover again and microwave on High (100 percent) for 5 to 7 minutes, stirring after 2½ to 3 minutes until the soup is heated through.

Pour the soup into 4 microwavable soup bowls. Lay 1 slice of melba toast on top of each serving of soup and sprinkle with 1 tablespoon of parmesan. Microwave on High (100 percent) for 2½ to 3 minutes until the cheese melts.

If you spill some soup when stirring it during cooking, don't worry; spatters and spills will not "bake" onto the oven walls. Microwave cleanup is easy and fast.

Seafood Gumbo

Serves 6

Gumbo, a savory stewlike soup, originated in Louisiana.

4 tablespoons (2 ounces) butter
10-ounce package frozen okra, defrosted and sliced
⅔ cup chopped scallions, including tops
½ cup chopped celery
2 teaspoons gumbo filé
2 teaspoons dried oregano
½ teaspoon pepper
½ teaspoon paprika
½ teaspoon dried thyme
¼ teaspoon hot pepper sauce
1 bay leaf
28-ounce can whole tomatoes, chopped,
*   juice reserved*
1½ cups water
½ pound peeled and cleaned shrimp
6 ounces crabmeat, drained and flaked
1½ cups cooked rice

Gumbo, to be considered the "real" thing, should contain okra or filé (dried sassafras), or both, as they thicken it to the correct consistency. The term "gumbo" comes from an African word for okra.

Combine the butter, okra, scallions, celery, filé, oregano, pepper, paprika, thyme, hot pepper sauce and bay leaf in a 3½-quart microwavable casserole. Cover and microwave on High (100 percent) for 4 to 5 minutes. Stir in the tomatoes, reserved juice and the water. Cover and microwave on High (100 percent) for 10 to 12 minutes until boiling, stirring every 4 minutes.

Add the shrimp and the crabmeat to the casserole. Cover and microwave on High (100 percent) for 4 to 7 minutes, stirring after 2 minutes, until the shrimp is just cooked. Remove the bay leaf.

Divide the rice between 6 soup bowls. Fill each with the gumbo and serve immediately.

Hearty Chicken Noodle Soup

Serves 10

Here is a truly substantial chicken noodle soup, like great-grandmother could make in a day or two. We can manage it in an hour with the help of the microwave.

3½-pound frying chicken
1 cup chopped carrots
1 cup chopped celery
1 onion, chopped
1½ cups uncooked noodles
4 teaspoons instant chicken bouillon
½ teaspoon dried marjoram
1 teaspoon salt
¼ teaspoon pepper
6 cups water
1 tablespoon finely chopped parsley

Put the chicken, breast side down, in a 4-quart microwavable casserole. Cover and microwave on High (100 percent) for 10 minutes. Turn the chicken breast side up, cover and microwave on High (100 percent) for 7 to 10 minutes, until the meat is tender and the juices run clear. Remove the chicken from the casserole.

Add the carrots, celery and onion to the casserole. Cover and microwave on High (100 percent) for 5 to 6 minutes until softened.

Remove the skin and bones from the chicken and cut the meat into bite-sized pieces.

Add the chicken, noodles, bouillon, marjoram, salt, pepper and water to the vegetables in the casserole. Cover and microwave on High (100 percent) for 20 to 25 minutes or until heated through, stirring after 10 minutes.

Sprinkle the parsley on the soup before serving.

New England Clam Chowder

Serves 4

Ask any Nor' Easterner—creamy New England clam chowder makes a first-rate lunch, especially if oyster crackers are on the table. Use freshly steamed or canned clams.

> *4 slices bacon, diced*
> *1 cup chopped onion*
> *1½ cups diced potatoes*
> *¼ cup water*
> *½ teaspoon salt*
> *2 cups milk*
> *2 tablespoons all-purpose flour*
> *¼ teaspoon dried thyme*
> *¼ teaspoon pepper*
> *⅛ teaspoon dried marjoram*
> *⅛ teaspoon dried oregano*
> *2 6½ ounce cans minced clams, with liquid*
> *1 tablespoon (½ ounce) butter*

Put the bacon in a 2½-quart microwavable casserole. Microwave on High (100 percent) for 3 to 4 minutes until the bacon is crisp. Remove the bacon from the casserole and drain it on paper towels. When cool, crumble the slices.

Add the onion to the bacon fat in the casserole. Cover and microwave on High (100 percent) for 3 minutes. Add the potatoes, water and salt. Cover and microwave on High (100 percent) for 10 to 12 minutes until the potatoes are tender.

Puree half the potato mixture, including the liquid, in a blender or food processor. Leave the other half in the casserole.

Combine the milk with the flour and add the mixture to the casserole with the thyme, pepper, marjoram, oregano, clams, butter, crumbled bacon and the pureed potatoes. Microwave on High (100 percent) for 4 minutes, stirring every minute, until the chowder is hot.

Tomato-Vegetable Soup

Serves 6 to 8

A tomato-rich soup packed with vegetables and great flavor. Add a salad and hot rolls for a satisfying meal.

> 6 medium-size tomatoes, peeled and chopped
> 2 cups water
> 10¾-ounce can condensed tomato soup
> 4 teaspoons chicken bouillon granules
> 1 tablespoon sugar
> ½ teaspoon dried basil
> ¼ teaspoon dried savory
> ⅛ teaspoon ground sage
> ⅛ teaspoon pepper
> ½ pound broccoli florets
> 2 cups cauliflower florets
> 1 medium-size onion, cut into ½-inch wedges
> 1 cup cooked rice

Glass covers hold in heat and moisture and are especially good when making soup. Transparent wrap is also a good covering, but not as effective as glass for long cooking.

Combine the tomatoes, water, tomato soup, bouillon granules, sugar and herbs. Cover and microwave on High (100 percent) for 30 minutes, stirring 2 or 3 times to break apart tomatoes.

Cut the broccoli and cauliflower stems into thin slices and break the florets into small pieces. Stir into the soup and add the onion. Cover and microwave on High (100 percent) for 15 to 20 minutes until the vegetables are tender. Stir once or twice during cooking. When heated through, add the cooked rice and serve.

Northern Bean Soup

8 to 10 servings

Even without the beef, this soup makes a tasty, protein-rich meal. As the recipe makes quite a large quantity of soup, you might want to freeze half the soup in a 1¼-quart microwavable container. To defrost, put the covered container in the microwave and cook on High (100 percent) for 10 to 20 minutes until heated through. Stir the soup 3 or 4 times during heating.

½ pound ground beef (optional)
8 slices bacon, cut into small pieces
1 medium-size onion, chopped
1 small green pepper, chopped
1 clove garlic, finely chopped
1½ cups cubed cooked ham
1 pound dried Great Northern beans, rinsed,
*   soaked overnight and drained*
6 cups hot water
¼ teaspoon pepper

Put the ground beef, if you are using it, in a 1¼-quart microwavable casserole. Cover and microwave on High (100 percent) for 2 to 4 minutes until the meat is no longer pink. Stir it once or twice to break it up. Drain the meat and set aside.

Combine the bacon, onion, green pepper and garlic in a 5-quart microwavable casserole. Microwave on High for 6 to 7 minutes until the green pepper is tender. Stir once or twice during cooking.

Add the ground beef, ham, dried beans, water and pepper. Cover and microwave on High (100 percent) for 15 to 20 minutes until boiling. Stir once during cooking.

Reduce the power to Medium (50 percent) and microwave for 1 to 1½ hours, until the beans are tender.

Freeze cooled soups in plastic Ziplock bags so that they lie flat in the freezer. Label them clearly—and date them. Never keep frozen soup longer than 3 months.

Stir 3 or 4 times during cooking. If the soup is too thick, add 2 or 3 cups of water.

Remove a cup of beans from the soup. Mash the beans and return to the soup. Stir and serve hot.

Speedy Potato Chowder

Serves 4

A filling and tasty way to use leftover chicken. The corn is an especially good addition.

> *4 slices bacon*
> *½ cup chopped onion*
> *10¾-ounce can condensed cream of potato soup*
> *1½ cups milk*
> *1 cup corn kernels*
> *1 cup diced cooked chicken*
> *2 tablespoons chopped parsley*

Put the bacon in a 2-quart microwavable casserole. Microwave on High (100 percent) for 3 to 4 minutes until crisp. Remove the bacon and drain it on paper towels. When cool, crumble the slices.

Pour off all but 1 tablespoon of bacon fat. Add the onion, cover, and microwave on High (100 percent) for 2 to 2½ minutes until softened.

Stir in the soup and milk. Add the corn, chicken, crumbled bacon and parsley and stir to combine. Cover the casserole and microwave on High (100 percent) for 8 to 10 minutes until heated through. Stir once or twice during cooking.

CHAPTER 2

FISH AND SEAFOOD

What is light, full of flavor, low in fat and fast and easy to prepare? The perfect food, of course—as every fish lover knows. Fish and seafood have long been favorites with cooks. Their fresh taste and pleasing texture can be coupled with so many side dishes and sauces that the appearance of the ocean's bounty is a welcome sight on any table, at almost any time of day.

The most important maxims of fish cookery are to buy it as fresh as possible and cook it as soon it as possible. This is where the microwave stars because it cooks fish and seafood quickly *and* perfectly. Fragile, delicate fish never becomes dry or chewy when cooked correctly in the microwave, and the uncomplicated sauces that enhance both fish and seafood are easily made in a microwave, too.

Lemon Fish Fillets

Serves 4

What could be easier than this recipe where the fish is "steamed" with wet paper towels? And with only three ingredients, it is a breeze to make.

4 3-ounce sole fillets
Lemon pepper seasoning
3–4 tablespoons lemon juice

Hold a paper towel under running water until soaked but not dripping. Put the wet towel on a microwavable plate or tray. Arrange the fillets on the towel with their thickest portions toward the outside.

Sprinkle each fillet with lemon pepper seasoning. Soak a second paper towel and lay it on top of the fish. Sprinkle the lemon juice over the paper towel. Microwave on High (100 percent) for 5 to 6½ minutes until the fish flakes. Rotate the dish once during cooking. Let the fish stand for 1 minute before serving.

FROZEN FISH

In almost every region of the country, fresh fish can be found, be it lake fish, river fish or ocean fish and seafood.

Still, there are times when only frozen is available and the microwave comes in very handy for defrosting and cooking. Microwave frozen fillets on Medium (50 percent) for 5 to 10 minutes a pound. Separate the fillets as quickly as you can and thaw them only until they are pliable. A pound of shrimp will thaw at Medium (50 percent) in about 5 to 8 minutes. Regardless of the kind of fish or seafood you are defrosting, rinse it in cold water and let it sit for 5 to 10 minutes after taking it from the microwave before you cook it.

Broiled Salmon

Serves 2

While not actually broiled, of course, this succulent salmon is an almost-instant dinner. Serve it with boiled potatoes tossed in butter and tender young green peas. If you are cooking for only one person, cook one salmon steak for 2 minutes before rotating it, and then for another 2 minutes after that.

> *4 tablespoons butter*
> *2 6-ounce salmon steaks*
> *4 teaspoons lemon juice*
> *2 parsley sprigs*
> *Salt and pepper*

Heat a microwavable ceramic browning tray on High (100 percent) for 3 minutes. Add 2 tablespoons of butter to the hot tray and lay the salmon steaks on top. Dot the steaks with the remaining butter. Sprinkle each one with lemon juice and top with a parsley sprig.

Microwave on High (100 percent) for 3 minutes. Rotate the dish a half turn and cook for another 3 to 4 minutes until the salmon flakes. Season to taste with salt and pepper.

Sole Florentine

Serves 4

A fillet of sole on a seasoned bed of spinach is a very
elegant and classical presentation.

2 10-ounce packages frozen chopped spinach
2 tablespoons finely chopped onion
½ teaspoon grated lemon rind
¼ teaspoon salt (optional)
¼ teaspoon pepper
½ teaspoon dry mustard
2 tablespoons grated parmesan cheese
1 tablespoon chopped parsley
½ teaspoon paprika
1 pound sole fillets
4 thin slices of lemon

When buying sole,
buy lemon, Rex,
gray sole or
nearly any fish
labeled "flounder"
fillets—whichever
seems freshest
and most
economical.

Pierce the packages of frozen spinach in several
places and microwave them on High (100 percent) for
6 minutes or until they flex easily. Rearrange them once
after 3 minutes. Drain the spinach well and put it in an
8-inch microwavable browning skillet (do not preheat
the skillet).

Add the onion, lemon rind, salt, pepper and mustard
to the spinach and stir well. Spread this mixture evenly
over the bottom of the skillet.

Lay the fish fillets on top of the spinach. Cover and
microwave on Medium (50 percent) for 3 minutes.
With a rubber spatula, rearrange the spinach and fish
around the edges of the skillet.

Combine the grated cheese, parsley and paprika.
Sprinkle this mixture over the fish. Cover the skillet
and microwave on Medium (50 percent) for 2 to 6
minutes until the fish flakes. Serve garnished with
lemon slices.

Haddock with Tomato Sauce

Serves 4

Use the freshest fish available and ripe, juicy tomatoes. The sauce is delicious on almost any firm-fleshed fish, and so quick to make.

4 medium-size tomatoes, cut into wedges
1 medium-size onion, chopped
2 tablespoons vermouth
1 tablespoon olive oil
1 teaspoon flour
2 teaspoons tomato paste
½ teaspoon dried thyme
½ teaspoon dried basil
Salt and pepper
2 pounds haddock
2 tablespoons butter, cut into pieces

Put all the ingredients except the haddock and butter in a microwavable casserole and stir to combine. Cover and microwave on High (100 percent) for 8 to 9 minutes until the sauce is heated through and the onion is very soft.

Puree the sauce in a blender or food processor and then strain to remove the tomato skins and seeds. Put the sauce back into the casserole and reserve while you cook the fish.

Dot the hadddock with butter and wrap it in wax paper. Put the wrapped fish in a 10-inch microwavable baking dish and microwave on High (100 percent) for 5 to 7 minutes until the fish flakes.

If necessary, reheat the sauce, uncovered, for a minute or two, and serve with the haddock.

Haddock is a small member of the cod family. Substitute hake, pollock or codfish for haddock in any recipe.

Swordfish with White Wine

Serves 4 to 6

Sweet, rich swordfish is a popular fish for grilling and
broiling, but it really does best in the microwave where
it never dries out or toughens. This method is simply
sensational.

> *2 pounds swordfish*
> *½ cup dry white wine*
> *1 tablespoon lemon juice*
> *4 scallions, finely chopped*
> *3 tablespoons finely chopped parsley*
> *2 tablespoons butter, cut into pieces*
> *Pepper*
> *Salt*

Remove the skin from the swordfish and put it in a
microwavable baking dish just large enough to hold it.
Pour the wine and lemon juice over the fish and sprinkle the surface with scallions and parsley. Dot with
butter and season with pepper.

Cover the baking dish with wax paper and microwave on Medium-High (70 percent) for 10 to 14 minutes until the fish flakes. Rotate the dish a quarter turn
every 2 to 4 minutes. Remove the fish from the microwave and season with salt. Let it stand for 5 minutes
before serving.

Beware of
overcooking
fish—cook it only
until it flakes, not
a minute longer.

Shrimp and Peppers

Serves 2

A great way to have beer-steamed shrimp in minutes. And with the paper towels there is virtually no cleanup.

> *½ pound medium-size fresh shrimp, shelled and deveined*
> *4 thin slices onion*
> *8 thin red pepper strips*
> *8 thin green pepper strips*
> *4 teaspoons butter, cut into pieces*
> *Cinnamon*
> *½ cup beer or water*

Lay 4 connected sheets of paper towels on the counter. Separate into 2 pieces, each of which has 2 connected sheets.

Put an equal amount of shrimp, onion slices and pepper strips on each paper towel directly over the perforations. Dot each serving with butter and then sprinkle each one with cinnamon. Fold both ends of the towels over the center of each serving of shrimp, over-lapping on the food.

Place the packets on a microwavable plate or tray, perforated side up. Pour ¼ cup beer evenly over each packet. Microwave on Medium-High (70 percent) for 2 to 4 minutes, or until the shrimp are firm. Let the packets stand for 2 minutes and then open them along the perforations.

Curried Shrimp

Serves 4

Curries can range from the simple to the very elaborate. Much of the pleasure of eating a curry is the variety of accompaniments, which include chutneys of every description, toasted coconut, pineapple cubes, raisins and nuts.

2 tablespoons vegetable oil
1 medium-size onion, chopped
½ green pepper, finely chopped
1 tablespoon curry powder
¼ teaspoon cumin
Dash cayenne pepper
2 tablespoons flour
1½ cups chicken broth
1 teaspoon lemon juice
1 tablespoon tomato paste
1½ pounds medium-size fresh shrimp, shelled
*   and deveined*

Pour the oil into a 1½-quart microwavable casserole and microwave on High (100 percent) for 30 seconds. Add the onion and green pepper and cook on High (100 percent) for 1 minute until the onion softens.

Stir in the curry powder, cumin and cayenne pepper and cook on High (100 percent) for 20 seconds. Stir in the flour, and then whisk in the chicken broth, lemon juice and tomato paste. Microwave on High (100 percent) for 3 minutes until heated through. Add the shrimp, stir and cook, uncovered, on High (100 percent) for 3 to 4 minutes until the shrimp are pink and just cooked through. Stir the shrimp once or twice during cooking so they will cook evenly.

CHAPTER 3

CHICKEN AND OTHER POULTRY

Nearly everyone likes to cook poultry because the relatively bland flavor blends with a variety of other ingredients to make dishes that can be elegant or simple, sauced or plain. What is more, skinned poultry is low in fat, calories and cholesterol, which is a boon for those who are on restricted diets. As if all this were not enough, poultry is relatively inexpensive and readily available, too.

Whenever you decide to cook chicken or another type of poultry, think of the microwave. Its speed and efficiency make cooking chicken or turkey so easy and leave it so moist and tender that you may never want to cook it by more conventional means again. Buy plump, fresh birds, if possible, and cook them soon after purchase. However, poultry will keep in the refrigerator for two or three days, if need be, particularly if well wrapped and placed near a back wall where the temperature is coldest. If you do freeze poultry, it is an easy matter to defrost it in the microwave. Freezing does alter its flavor and texture to some extent, though, so it is best to plan to serve a previously frozen bird cut up, with a tasty sauce.

Breaded Chicken

Serves 4

A good way to prepare chicken to serve warm for supper or to eat cold later as a snack or for lunch. Be sure to use unprinted paper towels, or better still, a brand developed exclusively for the microwave.

> *2½- to 3-pound broiler chicken, cut into 8 pieces*
> *and skinned*
> *⅔ cup seasoned bread crumbs*
> *1 tablespoon chopped parsley*
> *½ teaspoon salt*
> *¼ teaspoon pepper*
> *1 egg, beaten*
> *1 tablespoon vegetable oil*

Look for plump birds with snugly fitting skin. Be sure the breastbone is flexible and the cut joints, if any, look blood-red.

Rinse the chicken and pat it dry.

Combine the bread crumbs, parsley, salt and pepper on a plate. Mix the egg and oil in a shallow bowl. Dip the chicken pieces in the egg mixture and then roll them in the crumb mixture to coat.

Layer 4 sheets of paper towels on a 12-inch microwavable tray or platter. Arrange the chicken on top with the thickest portions toward the outside. Cover with a single layer of paper towels and microwave on High (100 percent) for 13 to 17 minutes until the chicken is no longer pink and the juices run clear. Let the chicken stand, covered, for 5 to 10 minutes before serving.

Hawaiian Chicken

Serves 4

If you are in a festive mood, this is a good dish to try. The pineapple's sweetness complements the garlic, scallions and peppers. Rice is a good accompaniment.

If you freeze poultry, defrost it in the microwave set on Low (30 percent). Allow 5 to 7 minutes to the pound for frozen chicken parts, Cornish hens and turkey parts. Unwrap the poultry first.

2 tablespoons vegetable oil
4 boneless chicken breast halves, skinned and
  cut into 1-inch pieces
2 cloves garlic, finely chopped
20-ounce can chunk pineapple, drained,
  juice reserved
3 tablespoons soy sauce
2 tablespoons white wine or sherry
¼ teaspoon powdered ginger
½ teaspoon salt
1 cup sliced celery
1 green pepper, cut into 1-inch pieces
2 scallions with tops, cut into 1-inch pieces
2 tablespoons cornstarch

Preheat a browning dish on High (100 percent) for 6 minutes. Carefully add the oil, chicken pieces and garlic, stirring to prevent them from sticking. Microwave on High (100 percent) for 2 to 3 minutes, stirring after 1 minute. Drain and discard the oil; set the chicken and garlic aside.

Combine the reserved pineapple juice, soy sauce, wine, ginger and salt in a 2-quart microwavable dish. Cover and microwave on High (100 percent) for 2 to 3 minutes. Add the pineapple chunks, celery, green pepper, scallions, chicken and garlic to the dish.

Combine the cornstarch with ¼ cup of water and stir into the vegetable and chicken mixture. Cover and microwave on High (100 percent) for 2 to 3 minutes, stirring after 1½ minutes, until the mixture is thickened and bubbly. Serve at once.

Broccoli-Stuffed Chicken Breast

Serves 2

To conjure up a little taste of the Far East, add sliced fresh ginger and a few drops of soy sauce to the mustard instead of the Italian seasoning.

> *1 whole boneless chicken breast, skinned, halved*
> *   and flattened*
> *2 teaspoons Dijon mustard*
> *1 teaspoon Italian seasoning*
> *4 3-inch spears fresh broccoli*

Rinse the chicken breast halves and pat them dry. Lay the breasts on the counter and spread each with a teaspoon of mustard. Sprinkle the seasoning over the breasts and arrange 2 broccoli spears on the center of each. Wrap the chicken breasts around the broccoli and secure with wooden toothpicks.

Lay each stuffed chicken breast on a wet paper towel. Wrap the chicken in the towel and lay on a microwavable plate or tray. Microwave on High (100 percent) for 4 to 6 minutes until the chicken is tender and thoroughly cooked. Let the stuffed breasts stand for 1 to 2 minutes before serving.

PAPER-TOWEL STEAMING

Use a paper towel for steaming foods such as vegetables, skinless poultry, fish and seafood. It is quick, easy— and there is no clean up. Put a single serving on a damp towel, wrap the towel round the food so that it is completely enclosed, and microwave on High (100 percent) for about 4 minutes. Or moisten the towel after the food is wrapped.

Chicken with Mushroom Sauce

Serves 8

An easy and elegant dish to prepare for your family or weekend guests.

> *4 boneless chicken breasts, skinned and cut in half*
> *3 ounces thinly sliced ham*
> *10¾-ounce can cream of mushroom soup*
> *½ cup sour cream*
> *1 cup sliced mushrooms*

Wrap a slice of ham around each chicken breast. Put the chicken in a 9-by-12-inch microwavable dish.

Combine the soup with the sour cream and pour the mixture over the chicken. Cover with transparent wrap, turning back one corner to vent. Microwave on High (100 percent) for 11 to 13 minutes. Rotate the dish a half turn and microwave on High (100 percent) for 5 to 7 minutes until the chicken is nearly cooked through.

Add the mushrooms to the dish and microwave, covered, on High (100 percent) for 4 to 5 minutes until the chicken is thoroughly cooked and the mushrooms are quite soft.

While the quest for a fresh chicken may seem overwhelming in this age of frozen poultry, try to buy chicken that has never been frozen.

Sweet-and-Sour
Cornish Hens

Serves 2

Cornish hens are tender and juicy when prepared in the microwave.

1 tablespoon (½ ounce) butter
½ cup finely chopped onion
1 teaspoon instant beef bouillon granules
¼ cup apricot preserves
¼ cup Russian dressing
2 Cornish hens (1–1½ pounds each)
¼ teaspoon salt

Put the butter in a 1-quart casserole and microwave on High (100 percent) for 30 to 45 seconds, until melted. Add the onion and microwave on High (100 percent) for 1 to 1½ minutes, until softened.

Stir in the beef bouillon and 1 tablespoon of water. Microwave on High (100 percent) for 1 to 1½ minutes, until the bouillon is dissolved. Stir in the preserves and the Russian dressing and microwave on High (100 percent) for 1 to 2 minutes, until melted.

Rinse the hens and pat them dry with paper towels. Sprinkle the cavities with salt and tie the legs together with thread or kitchen twine. Put the hens on a microwavable rack and brush them liberally with the sauce. Microwave on High (100 percent) for 15 to 20 minutes, rotating the hens on the rack every 5 minutes and brushing with sauce, until the meat on the inside of the legs is no longer pink and the juices run clear.

Remove the hens from the microwave, cover with foil and let stand for 5 minutes before serving.

Chicken Stir-Fry

Serves 4

A zesty stir-fry good enough for a special occasion and easy enough for every day.

¼ cup soy sauce
2 tablespoons vegetable oil
1 tablespoon dry sherry (optional)
2 whole boneless chicken breasts, skinned and
*   flattened*
1 medium-size green pepper, cut into ¼-inch strips
½ cup sliced almonds
1 medium-size onion, thinly sliced and separated
*   into rings*
2 cups hot cooked rice

Combine the soy sauce, oil and sherry in a bowl. Cut the flattened chicken into strips ¾ to 1½ inch long. Put these into the marinade and allow to marinate for 15 to 30 minutes at room temperature.

Heat a 10-inch browning skillet on High (100 percent power) for 5 minutes. Quickly and carefully put the chicken, the marinade, green pepper and almonds in the skillet. Stir until the sizzling subsides. Mix in the onion rings.

Microwave on High (100 percent) for 5½ to 8½ minutes until the chicken strips are tender and no longer pink. Stir every 2 minutes. Serve over hot rice.

Turkey and Broccoli Casserole

Serves 4

This combination of turkey and broccoli warmed in tangy, creamy sauce is also known as turkey divan.

3 tablespoons (1½ ounces) butter
3 tablespoons all-purpose flour
1 teaspoon instant chicken bouillon granules
⅛ teaspoon dry mustard
1½ cups milk
¼ cup mayonnaise
1 teaspoon lemon juice
2 cups broccoli florets
¾ pound cooked sliced turkey
2 tablespoons grated parmesan cheese

If you are buying turkey, look for a fresh one and get it a little larger than you need. Leftover turkey can be turned into any number of excellent dishes.

Put the butter in a 1-quart glass measure. Microwave on High (100 percent) for 30 seconds or until melted. Whisk in the flour, bouillon and mustard. Gradually stir in the milk. Microwave on High (100 percent) for 4 to 6 minutes, stirring every 2 minutes, until thickened. Stir in the mayonnaise and the lemon juice.

Put the broccoli in an 8-inch-square microwavable dish. Cover with transparent wrap, turning back one corner to vent. Microwave on High (100 percent) for 2 to 4 minutes until the broccoli is crisp-tender.

Arrange the turkey slices on top of the broccoli. Pour the sauce over the turkey and sprinkle with the parmesan cheese. Microwave on High (100 percent) for 5 to 6 minutes, or until thoroughly heated.

CHAPTER 4

BEEF

A juicy slice of roast beef, an aromatic piece of meatloaf, tender, tasty chunks of skewered beef —all are superb main courses. And beef is also delicious with dishes ranging from mashed or baked potatoes, steamed vegetables, crisp green salads and broiled tomatoes to rice pilaf and buttered noodles. No wonder we love beef. It tastes so good and often satisfies a hunger as no other meat does. Leftovers make unbelievably good sandwiches and cold meat salads, which help to stretch the beef budget.

Red meat cooked in the microwave may not brown and crisp the way it does in a conventional oven, and if the power is too high for too long, the natural juices will evaporate and leave the meat dry and tough. Despite these potential problems, beef can be cooked, very successfully, in the microwave. You will need to cook large pieces at a fairly low power—but they will cook beautifully in far less time than in a conventional oven. Ground meat and small cubes of beef are just right for microwave cooking, with tender, succulent results after only minutes.

Roast Beef

Serves 10

Roasts larger than four pounds should be cooked fat side down on a rack and turned over halfway through cooking. Shield the edges of the roast with small pieces of lightweight foil to prevent overcooking. To control spattering, cover the meat loosely with wax paper.

> *4-pound rolled beef rib roast*
> *Pepper*
> *Chopped fresh herbs such as thyme, rosemary*
> *or marjoram*

Season the roast with pepper or other herbs as desired, but do not salt.

Put the roast, cut side up, on a microwavable rack set in a shallow microwavable baking dish. Microwave on High (100 percent) for 5 minutes.

Cook on Medium (50 percent) for 15 minutes, rotating the dish once. Turn the roast over and continue cooking on Medium (50 percent) for 15 to 18 minutes. Insert a microwavable meat thermometer or probe into the center of the roast and cook until the desired temperature is reached: 120 degrees for rare, 135 degrees for medium and 150 degrees for well done.

Remove the roast from the oven, cover loosely with foil and let stand for 10 minutes before carving.

Use the probe that comes with many microwaves or a microwavable meat thermometer to gauge the internal temperature of a large cut of meat.

ROASTING MEAT IN THE MICROWAVE

Larger cuts of meat that are marbled and have a uniform shape microwave most successfully. If a roast is irregularly shaped, you may need to shield the smaller end with microwavable lightweight foil to prevent overcooking.

Pot Roast

Serves 6

When cooked in the microwave, pot roast is wonderfully succulent, very tender and takes about half the usual time. It is well worth planning ahead to allow plenty of time for marinating the meat.

> *3-pound boneless chuck steak or cross-cut shoulder of beef*
> *1½ cups red wine*
> *2 tablespoons vegetable oil*
> *1 medium-size onion, chopped*
> *1 clove garlic, chopped*
> *1 stalk celery, chopped*
> *1 teaspoon salt*
> *1 bay leaf*
> *1 teaspoon thyme*
> *3 sprigs parsley*
> *10 peppercorns*

Meat *without* the bone cooks more rapidly in the microwave than cuts with the bone left in.

Tie the beef at ½-inch intervals so it will keep its shape. Combine the remaining ingredients in a 2½-quart microwavable casserole. Put the beef in the casserole. (If there is not enough liquid to cover, be sure to turn it from time to time while it is marinating.) Cover the casserole and marinate the meat for 12 hours or up to 3 days in the refrigerator.

Put the beef, still immersed in the marinade and covered, in the microwave. Cook on Medium-Low (30 percent) for 45 minutes. Turn the beef over and cook on Medium-Low (30 percent) for 45 to 50 minutes longer. Rotate the dish every 20 minutes. Take the pot roast from the microwave and let it stand for 20 minutes before slicing.

Curry Beef Satay

Serves 4

This skewered beef dish is reminiscent of the satays made in many versions all around Southeast Asia. For more authentic flavor, substitute peanut oil for the vegetable oil.

> 2 tablespoons vegetable oil
> 2 tablespoons grated onion
> 1 tablespoon packed brown sugar
> 1 teaspoon curry powder
> 1 teaspoon soy sauce
> 2–3 drops hot pepper sauce
> 1¼ pounds beef top round steak, very thinly sliced
> 4 8-inch bamboo skewers
> Salt (optional)

Combine the oil, onion, sugar, curry, soy and pepper sauce in a large glass bowl and mix well. Add the beef, stir to coat, and let the mixture stand for 30 minutes.

Thread 2 to 3 slices of beef on an 8-inch wooden skewer. Thread the remaining meat on 3 more skewers until all the meat has been used. Put the skewers on a microwavable rack set in a shallow microwavable baking dish. Do not overcrowd the dish and arrange the skewers so that the meatier parts are facing the edge of the dish. If necessary, cook the meat in 2 batches with slightly reduced cooking times.

Brush the meat with any remaining curry mixture and microwave on High (100 percent) for 3 to 4 minutes, rotating the dish once. If desired, sprinkle lightly with salt just before serving.

Teriyaki Kabobs

Serves 4

Bottled sauces
such as soy,
Worcestershire,
steak sauce,
Kitchen Bouquet
and teriyaki sauce
add flavor and
also color the
meat during
microwave
cooking. They
often are referred
to as "browning
agents" or
"browning
sauces" in recipes
for the
microwave.

½ cup teriyaki sauce
2 tablespoons red wine
1 clove garlic, finely chopped
½ teaspoon powdered ginger
1 pound boneless sirloin steak, cut into
    ¼-inch strips
1 medium-size white onion, quartered and
    separated into layers
1 pint cherry tomatoes
1 large green pepper, cut into 1½-inch pieces
12 medium-size mushrooms
12 bamboo skewers

Combine the teriyaki sauce, wine, garlic and ginger in a bowl. Add the steak strips and stir to coat them, and marinate for 1 hour.

Skewer 2 strips of meat, 2 onion layers, 1 cherry tomato, 1 piece of green pepper, 1 mushroom and 2 more strips of meat on each skewer.

Put the skewers on a microwavable rack. Cover with transparent wrap and microwave on High (100 percent) for 1½ minutes. Turn the kabobs over. Cover again and microwave on High (100 percent) for 1½ to 2½ minutes. Let the kabobs stand for 2 to 3 minutes before serving.

Gingered Beef and Vegetables

Serves 2

A good beef recipe that uses the magical paper towel method for cooking.

> 2 tablespoons soy sauce
> 2 teaspoons vegetable oil
> ¼ teaspoon ground ginger
> Pepper
> ½ pound boneless sirloin steak, cut into ¼-inch strips
> 2 medium-size carrots, cut into thin 2-inch strips
> 1 small green pepper, cut into ¼-inch strips
> 4 tablespoons water

Blend the soy sauce, oil, ginger and pepper to taste in a small bowl. Stir in the sirloin strips and let them marinate for 15 minutes at room temperature.

Lay 4 sheets of paper towel on the counter, separated into 2 pieces so that each one has 2 connecting sheets. Lay an equal amount of carrot and pepper strips in the center of each piece of paper towel, directly over the perforations. Lift the sirloin strips from the marinade and divide them equally between the 2 portions on top of the vegetables.

Fold the long sides of the paper towels over the food and then fold over the ends to make an enclosed packet. Place the packets, perforated side up, on a microwavable plate or tray. Sprinkle each packet with 2 table-spoons of water and microwave on High (100 percent) for 5½ to 6½ minutes until the vegetables are crisp-tender. Open along the perforation to serve.

Meatloaf

Serves 2

It is possible to cook this old family standby in about 5 minutes when you use a microwave. As it is so easy, consider making two meatloaves and using the second for the next day's brown bag lunches.

½ pound ground beef
1 slice soft white bread, crumbled
2 tablespoons milk
1 tablespoon chopped onion
2 tablespoons ketchup
1 teaspoon Worcestershire sauce
½ teaspoon finely chopped garlic
⅛ teaspoon salt
Pepper

When cooking in a microwave, the shape of the cooking dish has a considerable effect on the cooking time. Food cooks most evenly in round dishes.

Crumble the beef in a bowl and mix in the crumbled bread, milk, onion, 1 tablespoon ketchup, the Worcestershire sauce, garlic, salt and pepper to taste. When the ingredients are well mixed, shape the meat into a loaf and put it in a small, oval microwavable casserole.

Microwave on High (100 percent) for 3 minutes, rotating a quarter turn after 1½ minutes. Brush the top of the meatloaf with the remaining tablespoon of ketchup. Microwave on High (100 percent) for 1 to 2½ minutes, until the internal temperature reaches 145 to 155 degrees. Rotate a half turn after half the cooking time. Let the meatloaf stand, uncovered, for 2 minutes.

CHAPTER 5

PORK, LAMB
AND VEAL

The "other" red meats are just as satisfying as beef and lend themselves to microwave cooking equally easily. Lamb and pork, both regional favorites, are not as nationally popular as beef, but they deserve to be. Their sweet, full-bodied flavors turn any meal into something out of the ordinary and they match especially well with fruit sauces, glazes and interesting vegetables. Pork is a winner when teamed with sweet potatoes, turnips or parsnips, and lamb is excellent served with eggplant, asparagus or lima beans. Both the light flavor and texture of tender young veal benefit greatly from gentle microwave cooking.

Buy meat from a reliable butcher or a well-stocked supermarket. Never hesitate to ask the butcher for advice or to ring for the meat man in the market when you are searching for a certain cut or size of meat. The meat should have a healthy reddish-pink color (veal will be the palest pink, followed by pork and then lamb) and should smell absolutely fresh. Cook the meat soon after you buy it, and, as is true of all microwave cooking, if it is cut into uniform pieces, it will cook evenly.

43

Tangy Marinated Pork Chops

Serves 4

A marinade is usually a combination of wine or vinegar with oil and condiments. The acid in the wine or vinegar tenderizes the meat. A meat marinade is often used to baste the meat while it is cooks, or as a base for a sauce.

The marinade in this recipe flavors and tenderizes the pork as it soaks overnight and then is combined with onion to make a tasty sauce for the chops.

½ cup plus 1 tablespoon vegetable oil
3 tablespoons steak sauce
3 tablespoons dry sherry
3 tablespoons red wine vinegar
1 tablespoon Worcestershire sauce
1 tablespoon packed brown sugar
1 teaspoon dried marjoram
4 pork loin chops, about 1 inch thick
1 medium-size onion, thinly sliced

Combine ½ cup of oil with the steak sauce, sherry, vinegar, Worcestershire sauce, brown sugar and marjoram in a 12-inch glass dish and stir until well mixed.

Put the pork chops in the dish and turn to coat with the marinade. Cover and let marinate for 8 hours or overnight, turning the chops occasionally.

Remove the chops from the marinade and pat dry with paper towels.

Heat a microwave browning dish on High (100 percent) for 6 minutes. Carefully add the remaining tablespoon of oil and the pork chops. Microwave on High (100 percent) for 1 minute on each side. Pour the marinade over the chops and top with the onion slices. Cover and microwave on Medium (50 percent) for 17 to 22 minutes, turning the chops over after 10 minutes, until the meat is tender and the juices run clear.

Barbecued Spareribs

Serves 2 to 4

There is no need to abandon your microwave on balmy summer evenings when outdoor grilling has its greatest appeal. Start the ribs off in the microwave but reduce the cooking time on Medium to 20 minutes. Remove from the bag and cook over hot coals for 30 minutes, turning frequently and brushing with sauce.

> *2 tablespoons cornstarch*
> *1 bunch scallions, chopped*
> *1 cup tomato sauce*
> *¼ cup tomato ketchup*
> *2 tablespoons cider vinegar*
> *2 tablespoons packed brown sugar*
> *1 teaspoon grated orange rind*
> *⅛ teaspoon ground cloves*
> *⅛ teaspoon pepper*
> *⅛ teaspoon salt*
> *⅛ teaspoon hot pepper sauce*
> *1 rack pork spareribs (about 3 pounds), cut into*
>   *4 portions*

Put all the ingredients in a 20-by-14-inch microwavable cooking bag. Gently squeeze the bag several times to combine the ingredients and moisten the ribs. Close the bag with the nylon tie provided, and gently press it into a microwavable baking dish, keeping the ribs in a single layer.

Make 6 ½-inch slits in the bag near the closure. Microwave on High (100 percent) for 8 minutes Then microwave on Medium (50 percent) for 40 to 45 minutes or until the ribs are tender, turning the bag once and rotating the dish twice. Let stand for 5 minutes.

Remove the meat from the cooking bag and cut into individual ribs. Pour the sauce that has accumulated out of the bag and serve with the ribs.

Red-Glazed Pork

Serves 6 to 8

Start cooking the rice on the stove top a few minutes before you begin microwaving the pork, and both will be ready to serve at about the same time.

3 tablespoons (1½ ounces) butter
1½ pounds pork tenderloin, thinly sliced and cut into strips
1 stalk celery, cut into ¼-inch diagonal slices
1 small green pepper, cut into ¼-inch strips
3 scallions, cut into ½-inch pieces
8-ounce can sliced water chestnuts
¼ cup soy sauce
2 tablespoons cornstarch
3 tablespoons tomato paste
2 tablespoons vinegar
3–4 cups hot cooked rice

Put the butter in a 10-inch covered microwave browning skillet. Microwave on High (100 percent) for 45 to 60 seconds until the butter is melted.

Add the pork, celery and green pepper and stir until coated. Cover and microwave on High (100 percent) for 6 to 10 minutes or until the pork is no longer pink, stirring 2 or 3 times.

Add the scallions and water chestnuts to the skillet. Cover again and set aside.

Combine the soy sauce, cornstarch, tomato paste and vinegar in a 1-quart microwavable measure, stirring until blended. Microwave on High (100 percent) for 1 to 3½ minutes or until thickened, stirring with a wire whisk every 30 seconds.

Slowly stir the sauce into the skillet. Microwave on High (100 percent) for 1 to 2 minutes or until heated through. Serve over hot cooked rice.

Broccoli-Sausage Stir-Fry

Serves 4

This is a truly multinational recipe, combining Oriental flavorings with homey vegetables and Polish sausage.

1½ cups thinly sliced carrots
1 cup chopped onion
2 cloves garlic, finely chopped
1 tablespoon vegetable oil
2 cups broccoli florets
½ pound cooked Polish sausage, sliced ½ inch thick
20-ounce can chunk pineapple, drained, juice reserved
¾ cup chicken broth
3 tablespoons soy sauce
1½ tablespoons cornstarch
½ teaspoon powdered ginger
2 cups hot cooked rice

Combine the carrots, onion, garlic and oil in a 2½-quart microwavable casserole. Cover and microwave on High (100 percent) for 2 to 4 minutes, until the carrots are just tender. Add the broccoli, cover again and microwave on High (100 percent) for 1 minute. Add the sliced sausage and microwave, covered, on High (100 percent) for 1 to 3 minutes, until the sausage is heated through. Stir in the pineapple chunks.

Combine the pineapple juice with the chicken broth, soy sauce, cornstarch and ginger in a microwavable bowl, stirring until the mixture is smooth. Microwave on High (100 percent) for 4 to 5 minutes, stirring every 2 minutes, until thickened and bubbly.

Pour the sauce over the sausage mixture. Cover and microwave on High (100 percent) for 2 to 3 minutes. Serve with hot cooked rice.

Veal Cacciatore

Serves 4

A tasty combination of tomatoes, herbs and cheese makes this veal dish special, yet it is easy enough for a weekday family meal.

> *8-ounce can whole tomatoes, chopped, juice reserved*
> *¼ cup chopped onion*
> *2 tablespoons red wine*
> *1 clove garlic, finely chopped*
> *½ teaspoon dried oregano*
> *½ teaspoon dried basil*
> *¼ teaspoon dried rosemary*
> *¼ teaspoon salt*
> *½ cup sliced mushroom*
> *½ cup chopped green pepper*
> *1 tablespoon all-purpose flour*
> *1 pound veal steak*
> *3 tablespoons bread crumbs*
> *3 tablespoons grated parmesan cheese*
> *1 tablespoon finely chopped fresh parsley*
> *¼ teaspoon Italian seasoning*
> *1 large egg, beaten*
> *2 tablespoons (1 ounce) butter*

Combine the chopped tomatoes and their juice with the onion, wine, garlic, oregano, basil, rosemary and salt in a 1½-quart microwavable bowl. Cover with transparent wrap, turning back one corner to vent. Microwave on High (100 percent) for 5 minutes, then stir in the mushrooms and peppers. Cover and cook on High for 5 more minutes.

Combine the flour with 2 tablespoons of water, stirring to make a smooth paste. Stir the flour mixture into the tomato sauce and microwave on High (100 percent) for 1 to 2 minutes, until thickened and bubbly. Cover with transparent wrap and reserve.

Cut the veal into 4 equal portions and pound each piece until it is about ¼ inch thick.

Combine the bread crumbs with the parmesan, parsley and Italian seasoning. Dip the pounded veal in the beaten egg and then in the crumb mixture, turning it until coated.

Put the butter in an 8-inch-square microwavable dish and microwave on High (100 percent) for 30 to 45 seconds, until melted. Put the veal in the dish and microwave on High (100 percent) for 2 to 3 minutes. Turn the meat over and microwave on High (100 percent) for 2 to 3 minutes more.

Remove the veal from the dish. Pour the reserved sauce into the dish and stir to mix it with the veal juices. Return the veal to the dish and microwave on High (100 percent) for 1 to 2 minutes to reheat.

East Indian Lamb and Eggplant

Serves 4

Lamb and eggplant are commonly thought of as a Greek combination, as in moussaka, but the spices in this recipe place it firmly in the realm of Indian cuisine. If you buy the small variety of eggplant, plan on serving eight slices. Otherwise four will be sufficient. You will also need a conventional broiler for this recipe.

> *1 pound lean lamb, cut into 1-inch slices*
> *1 cup canned tomatoes, finely chopped*
> *6-ounce can tomato paste*
> *½ teaspoon powdered ginger*
> *¼ teaspoon cinnamon*
> *4 scallions, chopped*
> *2 tablespoons finely chopped parsley*
> *1 teaspoon salt*
> *¼ teaspoon pepper*
> *4–8 slices eggplant, 1 inch thick*
> *4 tablespoons (2 ounces) butter, melted*
> *½ cup sour cream or plain yogurt*

Combine the lamb with the tomatoes, tomato paste, ginger, cinnamon, scallions, parsley, salt and pepper in a 2-quart microwavable casserole. Cover with wax paper and microwave on High (100 percent) for 8 to 9 minutes. Stir well, cover again and microwave on Medium (50 percent) for 20 to 25 minutes, or until the sauce is thickened and the lamb is tender. Remove from the microwave.

Preheat the broiler. Brush the eggplant slices with the melted butter and broil on both sides until browned.

To serve, arrange the eggplant on a warm serving platter. Divide the lamb mixture among the slices and top each with a spoonful of sour cream or yogurt.

Glazed Lamb Shoulder Roast

Serves 4 to 6

You do not need to use a microwave rack or trivet for this recipe—the ribs of the roast act as a rack to hold the meat out of its juice while it cooks.

> *4- to 6-pound lamb shoulder roast*
> *½ cup peach preserves*
> *¼ cup apricot nectar*
> *½ teaspoon powdered ginger*
> *1 tablespoon lemon juice*
> *1 clove garlic, finely chopped*
> *¼ teaspoon pepper*

Put the roast, rib side down, in a shallow microwave casserole. Combine the remaining ingredients in a small bowl and spread the glaze generously over the lamb.

Cover the roast with wax paper. Microwave on Medium (50 percent) for 9 to 10 minutes per pound for medium-rare, 10 to 11 minutes per pound for medium, or 11 to 12 minutes per pound for well done. Brush the roast with the glaze several times during cooking.

Remove the lamb from the microwave and let it stand, covered, for 10 to 15 minutes before serving.

MICROWAVE RACKS

Racks made specially for the microwave are often recommended for cooking larger cuts of meat, fish and poultry because they raise them above their juices so that they do not stew or overcook. Some dishes have built-in racks, or you can buy a separate rack to fit into a microwavable baking dish.

CHAPTER 6

VEGETARIAN MAIN COURSES

E ven if you are not a declared vegetarian, a meatless main course is a welcome change of pace. Vegetarian dishes usually are light and quick to make and combine a number of colorful ingredients with a range of flavors and textures. Best of all, they frequently are as kind to your pocketbook as they are to your health.

When you use the microwave to prepare vegetarian main courses (and there is no better place to cook vegetables), keep in mind that the firmer vegetables need to be partially cooked before they are mixed with moister, more tender specimens. The cooking time is so rapid that there is no chance for all the vegetables to cook completely unless they are treated in stages. Whenever possible, use seasonal, fresh ripe vegetables.

Eggs à la King

Serves 6

A delicious mushroom sauce envelops hard-cooked eggs for an imaginative light supper or lunch.

> *3 tablespoons (1½ ounces) butter*
> *½ cup sliced mushrooms*
> *2½ tablespoons all-purpose flour*
> *½ teaspoon dry mustard*
> *½ teaspoon instant chicken bouillon granules*
> *¼ teaspoon salt*
> *⅛ teaspoon pepper*
> *1¼ cups milk*
> *½ cup cooked peas*
> *4 hard-cooked eggs, sliced*
> *6 individual baked pastry shells*

Put 1 tablespoon of butter in a 2-quart microwavable casserole and microwave on High (100 percent) for 30 to 45 seconds until melted. Stir in the mushrooms and microwave on High (100 percent) for 1 to 2 minutes. Remove the mushrooms with a slotted spoon and set them aside.

Add the remaining butter to the casserole and microwave on High (100 percent) for 40 to 60 seconds, until melted. Stir in the flour, mustard, bouillon, salt and pepper. Gradually stir in the milk until smooth. Microwave on High (100 percent) for 2 to 4 minutes, stirring every minute, until the mixture is thickened.

Stir in the mushrooms, peas and egg slices. Microwave on High (100 percent) for 2 to 3 minutes until heated through. Spoon the mixture into the pastry shells and serve.

Never attempt to hard cook an egg in the microwave unless you have a special piece of microwave equipment designed for the task. Eggs in their shells may explode in the microwave.

Tofu Stir-Fry with Vegetables

Serves 4

Tofu, or bean curd, is high in protein and is available in health food stores and Asian vegetable markets and, frequently, at the supermarket. Its bland flavor and firm texture make it ideal for blending with snappier ingredients in a stir-fry.

> 1 pound firm tofu, drained
> ¼ cup soy sauce
> ¼ cup white wine
> 1 tablespoon vinegar
> 1 teaspoon sugar
> ½ teaspoon powdered ginger
> 1 tablespoon vegetable oil
> 1 cup thinly sliced carrots
> 4 scallions, cut into 1-inch pieces
> 1 cup sliced mushrooms
> 10 ounces snow pea pods
> 2 tablespoons cornstarch
> 2 cups hot cooked rice

It is important to turn back a corner of transparent wrap when microwaving vegetables to allow excess steam to escape.

Cut the tofu into 1-inch cubes. Combine the soy sauce, wine, vinegar, sugar and ginger in a glass bowl. Add the tofu and marinate for 8 hours or overnight. Drain the tofu in a colander, reserving the marinade in a 4-cup measure.

Put the oil in an 8-inch-square microwavable dish and microwave on High (100 percent) for 30 seconds. Add the carrots and cover with transparent wrap, turning back a corner to vent. Microwave on High (100 percent) for 1 to 2 minutes. Stir in the tofu, scallions, mushrooms and snow pea pods. Cover and microwave on High (100 percent) for 2 minutes.

Mix the cornstarch with 2 tablespoons of water, stirring to make a smooth paste. Stir this into the reserved marinade. Microwave on High (100 percent) for 3 to 5 minutes, stirring every minute, until the sauce is thickened and bubbly.

Pour the sauce over the tofu mixture. Cover and microwave on High (100 percent) for 1 to 2 minutes, until heated through. Serve with hot cooked rice.

Rice-Stuffed Peppers

Serves 4

> 4 large green peppers
> 3 cups cooked long grain and wild rice mix
> 1 cup cooked peas
> 2½ tablespoons chopped fresh dill
> 2 medium-size tomatoes, cut into wedges
> ½ teaspoon dried oregano
> ¼ teaspoon dried basil
> 1 tablespoon olive oil

Cut a thin slice from the bottom of each pepper so that it will stand upright. Slice off the tops of the peppers and scoop out the ribs and seeds.

Stand the peppers in an 8-inch-square microwavable dish. Cover with transparent wrap, turning back one corner to vent. Microwave on High (100 percent) for 3 to 5 minutes until softened.

Combine the rice with the peas and 2 tablespoons of the dill. Spoon the mixture into the peppers. Stand a pepper in each corner of the dish and arrange the tomato wedges between them. Sprinkle the peppers with the oregano, basil and the remaining dill. Drizzle the olive oil over the tomatoes. Cover the dish with transparent wrap, turning back one corner to vent. Microwave on Medium-High (70 percent) for 8 to 12 minutes, rotating the dish a half turn after 4 minutes, until the peppers are tender and the filling is hot.

Scooped-out peppers need to be cooked before they are stuffed so that they will be tender when their filling is heated through.

Spinach Lasagne

Serves 8

This cheese-rich version of lasagne is made with spinach filling (not spinach pasta) and is a good choice when you need to plan and prepare ahead. It can go directly from the refrigerator to the microwave, completely assembled.

15½-ounce jar meatless spaghetti sauce
⅓ cup water
1 teaspoon dried oregano
½ teaspoon dried basil
1 tablespoon fresh chopped parsley
½ teaspoon salt
5 ounces uncooked lasagne noodles
1½ cups ricotta cheese
10-ounce package frozen chopped spinach, thawed
2 cups grated mozzarella cheese
⅓ cup grated parmesan cheese

Combine the spaghetti sauce with the water, oregano, basil, parsley and salt. Pour one third of the mixture into the bottom of an 8-inch-square microwavable dish. Lay half the lasagne noodles over the sauce.

Spread ¾ cup ricotta cheese, half the spinach and 1 cup mozzarella cheese over the noodles. Pour half the remaining sauce over the top.

Layer the remaining lasagne, ricotta, spinach and mozzarella over the sauce, in that order. Pour the remaining sauce on the top and sprinkle with the parmesan cheese.

Cover the dish with a double layer of transparent wrap. Chill for several hours or overnight. Microwave on Medium (50 percent) for 25 to 35 minutes or until the noodles are tender. Let the dish stand for 5 to 10 minutes before serving.

Fried Rice with Vegetables

Serves 4

This recipe tastes so authentic that you could almost believe it was made in a Chinese restaurant kitchen. Fried rice is very simple to make and pleases children and adults alike.

> ⅓ cup thinly sliced celery
> ⅓ cup chopped green pepper
> ⅓ cup chopped scallions
> 1 small carrot, chopped
> 8-ounce can bamboo shoots, drained
> 8-ounce can water chestnuts, sliced or
> ¼ cup sliced almonds (optional)
> 2 tablespoons vegetable oil
> 1 tablespoon chopped fresh parsley
> ⅛ teaspoon salt
> ⅛ teaspoon pepper
> 3 tablespoons soy sauce
> 2 large eggs, lightly beaten
> 2 cups cooked rice

Combine the celery, green pepper, scallions, carrot, bamboo shoots and optional water chestnuts or almonds in a bowl. Stir in the oil, parsley, salt and pepper.

Heat a 10-inch microwave browning dish on High (100 percent) for 3 minutes. Add the soy sauce all at once. Add the vegetable mixture, stir and cover. Microwave on High (100 percent) for 2 to 4 minutes, until the vegetables are crisp-tender.

Put the eggs in a microwavable bowl. Microwave on High (100 percent) for 1 to 1¼ minutes or until the eggs are almost set, stirring after 40 seconds.

Add the eggs and rice to the vegetable mixture and stir thoroughly. Microwave on High (100 percent) for 2 minutes, stirring after 1 minute, until heated through.

Cheese and Spinach Pie

Serves 4 to 6

A first-rate spinach dish that is wonderful served with a light, lemon-dressed salad.

> *10-ounce package frozen chopped spinach*
> *¼ cup finely chopped onion*
> *9-inch deep-dish pie shell, baked and put in a*
> *   microwavable dish*
> *1 cup (4 ounces) grated Swiss cheese*
> *3 large eggs*
> *⅔ cup evaporated milk*
> *½ teaspoon salt*
> *⅛ teaspoon ground nutmeg*
> *⅛ teaspoon cayenne pepper*
> *¼ cup grated parmesan cheese*

Put the spinach and onion in a 1-quart microwavable dish. Cover with transparent wrap, turning back one corner to vent. Microwave on High (100 percent) for 6 minutes, stirring once. Drain thoroughly in a colander, pressing to extract the moisture.

Spread half the spinach mixture over the bottom of the pie shell. Top with ½ cup of the Swiss cheese. Repeat the layers with the remaining spinach and Swiss cheese.

Beat together the eggs, evaporated milk, salt, nutmeg and cayenne. Pour the mixture over the layers in the pie shell and sprinkle the parmesan cheese over the top. Microwave on Medium (50 percent) for 10 to 12 minutes or until the filling is set, turning the dish after 5 minutes. Let stand for 10 minutes before serving.

Mixed Vegetables with Pasta

Serves 4 to 6

Crisp vegetables in a creamy sauce are an elegant, savory topping for hot pasta.

The more uniformly shaped and cut vegetables are, the more evenly they will cook.

1½ cups thinly sliced carrots
2 medium-size zucchini, cut into 2-by-⅛-inch strips
2 cups cauliflower florets
1 cup mushrooms, cut into quarters
5 tablespoons (2½ ounces) butter
½ teaspoon salt
2 tablespoons finely chopped onion
1 tablespoon all-purpose flour
⅛ teaspoon pepper
1 cup milk
2 tablespoon grated parmesan cheese
3 tablespoons chopped parsley
½ pound linguine or spaghetti, cooked and drained

Arrange the carrots around the outside of a 12-inch round microwavable platter. Make a circle of cauliflower and zucchini strips in alternating groups inside the carrot border. Put the mushrooms in the center of the platter.

Put 2 tablespoons of the butter in a glass measure and microwave on High (100 percent) for 30 to 40 seconds until melted. Combine the melted butter with ¼ teaspoon of the salt and spoon the mixture over the vegetables. Cover with transparent wrap, turning back one corner to vent. Microwave on High (100 percent) for 7 to 11 minutes, rotating the platter after 4 minutes. Let the vegetables stand, still covered, for 2 minutes before testing for doneness—they should be crisp-tender.

To make the sauce, put 2 tablespoons of butter in a

1-quart microwavable measure. Microwave on High (100 percent) for 30 to 45 seconds or until melted. Stir in the onion and microwave on High (100 percent) for 1 minute, until the onion is softened. Stir in the flour, the remaining salt and the pepper. Add the milk gradually, stirring until the mixture is smooth. Microwave on High (100 percent) for 3 to 5 minutes, stirring every minute, until the sauce is thickened. Stir in 1 tablespoon of the cheese and 2 tablespoons of parsley.

Toss the pasta with the remaining butter, cheese and parsley. Spoon the vegetables over the pasta and top with the sauce.

RICE AND PASTA TIPS

COOKING RICE IN THE MICROWAVE

For 1 cup of rice, combine $1/3$ cup rice with $2/3$ cup water in a large microwavable casserole, cover and cook it on High (100 percent) for 3 to 5 minutes or until boiling. Reduce the heat to Medium (50 percent) and cook it for 5 to 7 minutes longer until the water is absorbed.

COOKING AND REHEATING PASTA

When a recipe calls for conventionally cooked pasta to serve with a microwaved sauce, cook the pasta while you prepare the sauce. If necessary, cooked pasta can be reheated in the microwave without any loss of texture or flavor.

CASSEROLES AND STEWS

Qne-dish meals such as stews and casseroles are long-time favorites with cooks. This is hardly surprising because they meet so many requirements: they can be made ahead of time, store easily, frequently use inexpensive ingredients, can use leftovers to their best advantage, do not demand a lot of side dishes, reheat nicely the next day and they taste *really* good.

While most stews and casseroles are simple to make in a conventional oven or on the stove top, using the microwave to cook them has more advantages than the instantly appreciated fact that it saves time. When cooked in the microwave, the individual ingredients in a dish retain their own identity because they cook so quickly and evenly. Seasonings are a bit more intense because of the short cooking time too, so there is less reason to repeatedly taste and season.

And when it comes to reheating, no need to add liquid or transfer the casserole into a smaller container. Just pop the dish in the microwave for a few minutes and enjoy your own good food—even with microwave magic, stews and casseroles taste better the second day.

Beef Stew

Serves 4

Tapioca serves as a useful thickener in a microwaved stew.

> *1 pound lean beef, cut into 1-inch cubes*
> *2 medium-size onions, cut in quarters*
> *2 stalks celery, sliced diagonally*
> *3 carrots, peeled and sliced diagonally*
> *2½ tablespoons quick-cooking tapioca*
> *1½ teaspoons salt*
> *¼ teaspoon pepper*
> *¼ teaspoon dried basil*
> *¼ cup red wine*
> *1½ cups tomato juice*
> *1 large potato, peeled and diced*

Combine all the ingredients, except the potato, in a 2½-quart microwavable casserole. Cover and microwave on High (100 percent) for 4 minutes. Microwave, covered, on Medium (50 percent) for 10 minutes, stirring after 5 minutes.

Add the potato to the casserole. Cover and microwave on Medium (50 percent) for 20 to 30 minutes, until the meat and vegetables are tender, stirring every 5 minutes.

Turkey Bourguignon

Serves 6

When you have a sizable amount of roast turkey left over, make this robust stew. The last thing it will remind you of is "leftover" anything!

> *2 slices bacon*
> *3 tablespoons (1½ ounces) butter*

3 scallions, thinly sliced
1 clove garlic, finely chopped
½ pound button mushrooms, trimmed
2 tablespoons all-purpose flour
½ cup red wine
½ cup beef broth
2 tablespoons brandy
2 teaspoons Worcestershire sauce
½ teaspoon dried thyme
⅛ teaspoon pepper
1½ pounds cooked turkey, cut into ¾-inch pieces
3 cups hot cooked rice or noodles

Put the bacon on a double thickness of paper towels on a microwavable rack. Cover with paper towels and microwave on High (100 percent) for 1½ to 2 minutes until brown and crisp. When it is cool enough to handle, crumble the bacon.

Put 2 tablespoons of the butter in a 2½-quart microwavable casserole and microwave on High (100 percent) for 40 to 50 seconds, until melted. Stir in the scallions, garlic and crumbled bacon. Microwave on High (100 percent) for 1 minute. Add the mushroom caps and microwave on High (100 percent) for 2 to 3 minutes. Remove the bacon and vegetables from the casserole with a slotted spoon and set them aside.

Add the remaining butter to the casserole and microwave on High (100 percent) for 30 to 40 seconds. Stir in the flour and microwave on High (100 percent) for 1½ minutes. Stir in the wine, broth, brandy, Worcestershire sauce, thyme and pepper. Microwave on High (100 percent) for 3 to 5 minutes, until the sauce is thickened and bubbly.

Stir the turkey into the sauce. Cover and microwave on High (100 percent) for 5 to 7 minutes until the turkey is hot. Stir the bacon and vegetables into the casserole and microwave on High (100 percent) for 1 to 2 minutes. Serve the casserole over hot cooked rice or noodles.

A dish designated "Bourguignon" includes red wine and, usually, bacon, onions and mushrooms among its ingredients. The classic such dish is Beef Bourguignon, created in the Burgundy region of France.

Belgian Chicken Casserole

Serves 4

This traditional recipe from Belgium, known there as "Waterzooi," is a cross between a substantial soup and a delicate stew. It is best served in shallow bowls.

> *3-pound chicken, cut into serving pieces*
> *Pepper*
> *3 tablespoons (1½ ounces) butter*
> *4 leeks, sliced, or 2 onions, finely chopped*
> *2 stalks celery, sliced*
> *2 carrots, sliced*
> *2 cups chicken broth*
> *2 large egg yolks*
> *2 tablespoons milk or light cream*
> *3 tablespoons finely chopped parsley*
> *1 teaspoon salt*

Season the chicken pieces with pepper to taste.

Put the butter in a 2½-quart microwavable casserole and microwave on High (100 percent) for 40 to 60 seconds, until melted. Put the vegetables in the bottom of the casserole and set the chicken pieces on top of the vegetables. Add the chicken broth. Cover and cook on Medium-High (70 percent) for 30 to 35 minutes until the chicken is cooked.

Take out the chicken and, when it is cool enough to handle, remove and discard the skin.

Combine the egg yolks and milk or cream thoroughly and stir into the casserole. Return the chicken to the casserole and microwave on High (100 percent) for 2 to 3 minutes, until the sauce is lightly thickened and the chicken is hot. Stir in the parsley and salt and serve immediately.

Ground Beef and Noodles

Serves 4

Ground beef dishes cook quickly in the microwave and will continue to cook for a few minutes during standing—so do not taste for doneness until the casserole has "stood" for a few minutes.

1 pound ground chuck
1 tablespoon vegetable oil
1 onion, finely chopped
1 clove garlic, finely chopped
1 green pepper, stemmed, seeded and chopped
½ teaspoon dried oregano
¼ cup beef broth
¾ cup sour cream
1 tablespoon tomato paste
2 tomatoes, peeled, seeded and chopped
1½ cups cooked noodles or macaroni
½ teaspoon salt
⅛ teaspoon pepper

Heat a microwave browning dish on High (100 percent) for 4 minutes. Add the beef and oil and cook on High (100 percent) for 2 minutes. Drain off the fat and transfer the beef to a 2-quart microwavable casserole.

Add the onion, garlic and green pepper to the casserole and microwave on High (100 percent) for 2 to 3 minutes, until the vegetables are softened.

Add all the remaining ingredients to the casserole and stir to combine. Cover and microwave on High (100 percent) for 5 to 6 minutes, stirring the mixture and rotating the dish a quarter turn after 3 minutes. Let the casserole stand for 5 minutes before testing for doneness. Season with salt and pepper.

Standing time is often an important part of microwave cooking. After the food is removed from the oven, it continues to cook by transfer of its internal heat.

Lamb Stew

Serves 6

Worcestershire
sauce has the dual
role of acting as a
browning agent
for the meat while
contributing
distinctive flavor.

1¼ pounds boned leg of lamb, cut into 1-inch pieces
1 teaspoon Worcestershire sauce
18-ounce can tomatoes, drained and chopped
2 tablespoons cornstarch
¼ cup water
1 teaspoon dried thyme
1 teaspoon salt
1 medium-size onion, cut into quarters
1 clove garlic, finely chopped
½ cup chopped celery
6 small carrots, peeled, cut in quarters lengthwise
*   and cut in half crosswise*
4 small potatoes, peeled and cut into quarters
10-ounce package frozen peas

Put the lamb, Worcestershire sauce and tomatoes in
a 3-quart microwavable casserole and stir to combine.
Cover and microwave on High (100 percent) for 10
minutes, stirring after 5 minutes.

Combine the cornstarch with the water, stirring until
smooth. Stir the cornstarch into the meat. Add the
thyme and salt. Cover the casserole and let it stand.

Put the onion and garlic in a 1½-quart microwavable
casserole. Cover and microwave on High (100 percent)
for 1 minute. Add the celery, carrots and potatoes to the
casserole. Cover and microwave on High (100 percent)
for 10 to 12 minutes, stirring after 5 minutes, until the
vegetables are tender.

Add the vegetables to the lamb in the 3-quart casserole. Stir in the peas. Cover and microwave on High
(100 percent) for 12 to 15 minutes, stirring every 3
minutes, until the sauce is thickened. Let the stew stand
for 10 minutes before serving.

Lamb and Rice Casserole

Serves 6

Lamb and stuffed green olives are an awfully good combination—as the Greeks have long known.

1 pound lean lamb, cut into ¾-inch pieces
6-ounce package long grain and wild rice with
*   herbs*
1 onion, finely chopped
1 cup sliced mushrooms
2½ cups beef broth
¼ teaspoon cayenne pepper
½ cup chopped stuffed green olives
⅓ cup grated parmesan cheese

Put the lamb in a 2½-quart microwavable casserole. Add the rice, onion, mushrooms, broth and cayenne. Cover and microwave on High (100 percent) for 5 minutes. Stir and microwave on Medium-High (70 percent) for 30 to 35 minutes.

Stir the olives into the casserole. Microwave on High (100 percent) for 2 to 3 minutes. Sprinkle the parmesan cheese on top, cover and let stand for 3 minutes before serving.

DEFROSTING

Casseroles are handy make-ahead dishes because they freeze so well. When you want to defrost them, do so in the microwave on a Low setting (sometimes labeled "defrost"). The Low setting (30 or 50 percent) allows time during "off periods" for the heat to equalize within the food so that it defrosts evenly.

Tuna Casserole

Serves 4

This casserole is always a good standby for lunch or supper and it reheats well.

> *3 tablespoons (1½ ounces) butter*
> *½ cup chopped celery*
> *½ cup chopped onion*
> *¼ cup chopped green pepper*
> *½ cup sliced mushrooms*
> *3 tablespoons all-purpose flour*
> *2 teaspoons Dijon mustard*
> *2 teaspoons chopped fresh dill*
> *¼ teaspoon salt*
> *⅛ teaspoon cayenne pepper*
> *1 cup milk*
> *1 cup small-curd cottage cheese*
> *6½-ounce can water-packed tuna, drained*
> *2 cups cooked noodles*

Put the butter in a 2-quart microwavable casserole. Microwave on High (100 percent) for 30 to 45 seconds or until melted. Add the celery, onion, green pepper and the mushrooms. Cover and microwave on High (100 percent) for 3 minutes. Add the flour, mustard, dill, salt and cayenne.

Gradually stir in the milk and the cottage cheese. Microwave, uncovered, on High (100 percent) for 5 minutes, stirring twice.

Stir in the tuna and the cooked noodles. Microwave on High (100 percent) for 6 to 8 minutes, stirring once.

Pizza Casserole

Serves 6

One of the great things about pizza is the combination of many different flavors. Why not re-create such a successful formula in a casserole?

1 pound ground beef
½ cup chopped onion
⅓ cup chopped green pepper
1 clove garlic, finely chopped
1¼ cups uncooked macaroni
1 cup water
15-ounce jar pizza sauce
¼ pound mushrooms
¼ pound sliced pepperoni
1 cup grated mozzarella cheese
¼ cup grated parmesan cheese

Combine the beef, onion, green pepper and garlic in a 3½-quart microwavable casserole. Microwave, uncovered, on High (100 percent) for 5 to 6 minutes. Drain off and discard the fat.

Add the macaroni, water, pizza sauce and the mushrooms. Cut the pepperoni slices in half and add them to the casserole. Stir to combine the ingredients and microwave, covered, on High (100 percent) for 15 to 18 minutes, stirring every 5 minutes.

Sprinkle the mozzarella and parmesan cheeses over the casserole. Cover and allow to stand for 5 to 10 minutes before serving.

CHAPTER 8

SAVORY PIES
AND TARTS

Like casseroles and stews, savory pies and pizzas satisfy a certain hunger, in that they are fairly hearty and full of a delicious tumble of flavors. But pies and tarts are, by nature, more defined and refined. Often a firm filling is encased in a delicate crust, or a more robust pastry tops a bubbling-hot mixture of cheese and meat, vegetables and egg.

Because of the crust, many savory pies and tarts—open-faced, flat and covered—should be served immediately after they are cooked so that the crust has no time to turn soft and soggy. Sometimes you can cook the crusts in the microwave, at other times they are better when partially baked (without filling) in a conventional oven, cooled and then filled before being put in the microwave. Follow the instructions in the individual recipe.

If you prefer, you can buy the pastry dough in the frozen or refrigerated sections of the supermarket—it is quite good and suitable for these recipes. If not, make your own following a favorite recipe. Just be sure the pastry you choose is not sweet.

Cheddar, Bacon and Egg Pie

Serves 6

For a light supper or quick lunch, this crustless cheese and egg pie will hit the spot.

> *3 slices bacon*
> *¼ cup chopped onion*
> *2 cups unflavored croutons*
> *1 cup grated cheddar cheese*
> *4 large eggs*
> *2 cups half-and-half*
> *½ teaspoon salt*
> *½ teaspoon Dijon mustard*
> *⅛ teaspoon pepper*

Put the bacon on a double thickness of paper towel on a microwavable rack and cover with a paper towel. Microwave on High (100 percent) for 2½ to 3½ minutes, until the bacon is crisp.

Put the onion in a small microwavable dish. Cover and microwave on High (100 percent) for 45 seconds to 1 minute, until it is softened.

Combine the croutons and the cheese in an 8¼-inch round microwavable dish.

Whisk together the eggs, half-and-half, salt, mustard and pepper. Stir in the onion. Pour the mixture over the croutons and cheese. Crumble the bacon and sprinkle it over the top. Microwave on Medium (50 percent) for 20 to 25 minutes, until a knife inserted in the center comes out clean.

The amount of time needed to cook bacon in the microwave varies according to the thickness of the slices. Generally speaking, thin-sliced bacon microwaves more successfully than thick-sliced.

Chicken Pot Pie

Serves 6 to 8

Flavorful chicken pot pie is often topped with biscuit dough or overlapping rounds of pie dough.

> *3¾ cups chicken broth*
> *1 cup thinly sliced carrots*
> *1 cup chopped onion*
> *1 cup chopped celery*
> *1 cup diced potato*
> *¼ teaspoon pepper*
> *½ teaspoon dried thyme*
> *1 cup fresh or frozen peas*
> *¼ cup milk*
> *⅓ cup all-purpose flour*
> *2 cups diced cooked chicken*
> *Dough for 9-inch pie*
> *1 tablespoon (½ ounce) butter, melted*

Put 3½ cups of the broth in a 2-quart microwavable casserole. Add the carrots, onion, celery, potato, ¼ teaspoon thyme and the pepper. Stir well and microwave, covered, on High (100 percent) for 12 to 16 minutes, stirring every 3 minutes, until the vegetables are tender. Stir in the peas.

Combine the remaining ¼ cup of broth with the milk and the flour, stirring until smooth. Stir the mixture into the casserole and microwave on High (100 percent) for 4 to 6 minutes, until the sauce is thickened and bubbly.

Stir the chicken into the casserole. Microwave on High (100 percent) for 2 to 3 minutes, until the chicken is heated through. Remove the mixture from the microwave and keep warm.

Roll the dough out flat on a lightly floured countertop. Cut it into 2- to 3-inch circles, using a cookie cutter or an inverted glass. Put the circles on a sheet of wax paper. Brush with the melted butter and sprinkle with the remaining ¼ teaspoon of thyme. Microwave on High (100 percent) for 2 to 3 minutes until the pastry is cooked and no longer doughy.

Cover the chicken filling with the pastry, overlapping the circles to fit, and serve at once.

Broccoli-Cheddar Pie

Serves 4

10-ounce package frozen chopped broccoli
¼ cup chopped scallion
9-inch deep-dish pie shell, baked
1 cup (4 ounces) grated cheddar cheese
3 large eggs
⅔ cup half-and-half
½ teaspoon salt
⅛ teaspoon nutmeg
Cayenne pepper
¼ cup grated parmesan cheese

Put the broccoli and scallion in a 1-quart microwavable dish. Cover with transparent wrap, turning back one corner to vent. Microwave on High (100 percent) for 6 minutes, stirring once. Drain thoroughly.

Spread half the broccoli mixture over the bottom of the pie shell. Sprinkle with half the cheese. Repeat the layers with the remaining broccoli and cheese.

Whisk together the eggs and the half-and-half. Stir in the salt, nutmeg and cayenne to taste. Pour the liquid over the broccoli and cheese and microwave on Medium (50 percent) for 10 to 12 minutes, until set, rotating the dish a half turn after 5 minutes. Let the pie stand for 10 minutes before serving.

Savory Beef Pie

Serves 6

Pie dough that will line the bottom of a moist pie such as this one can be cooked very successfully in the microwave as it does not need to brown.

> *Dough for a 9-inch pie*
> *¼ cup chopped onion*
> *1 pound lean ground beef*
> *½ cup grated carrots*
> *⅓ cup dry bread crumbs*
> *⅓ cup ketchup*
> *¼ cup evaporated milk*
> *½ teaspoon salt*
> *½ teaspoon oregano*
> *⅛ teaspoon pepper*
> *1 cup grated cheddar cheese*
> *1 teaspoon Worcestershire sauce*

Fit the pie dough into a 9-inch microwavable pie plate and prick the bottom with a fork. Cover with a paper towel. Put the pie plate in the microwave on an inverted microwavable saucer. Microwave on High (100 percent) for 4 minutes, rotating the dish a half turn after 2 minutes.

Put the onion in a small microwavable bowl. Cover with transparent wrap and microwave on High (100 percent) for 1 minute to soften.

Combine the onion with the beef, carrots, bread crumbs, ketchup, milk, salt, oregano and pepper in a large bowl. Spoon the mixture into the pie shell. Microwave on High (100 percent) for 8 to 10 minutes, rotating the pie a half turn after 4 minutes. If the filling is pulling away from the shell, press it back gently with a spoon.

Combine the cheese with the Worcestershire sauce

and sprinkle the mixture over the top of the pie. Micro-wave on High (100 percent) for 2 to 3 minutes, until the cheese is melted. Let the pie stand for 5 to 10 minutes before serving.

Tortilla Stacks

Serves 4

Layers of mildly spicy beef sandwiched between tortillas makes an easy deep-dish pie.

> *1 pound ground beef*
> *½ cup chopped onion*
> *16-ounce can tomato sauce*
> *1½-ounce package chili seasoning mix*
> *½ cup sliced black olives*
> *6 corn tortillas*
> *2 cups grated cheddar cheese*

Combine the beef and onion in a 1½-quart microwavable dish. Microwave on High (100 percent) for 5 to 8 minutes, until browned. Drain the meat in a colander and return it to the dish.

Stir in the tomato sauce, the chili seasoning mix and the black olives. Cover and microwave on High (100 percent) for 5 to 6 minutes, stirring after 2 minutes.

Layer the tortillas, the meat sauce and 1½ cups of the grated cheese in a round 2-quart microwavable casserole. Cover and microwave on High (100 percent) for 9 to 12 minutes, turning the dish every 4 minutes, until the tortillas are tender.

Remove the cover from the casserole. Top the tortillas with the remaining ½ cup of cheese. Allow the dish to stand for 5 minutes. Cut into wedges to serve.

A tortilla is a thin flat pancake made from unleavened corn or wheat flour. You can serve them plain, heated with butter or with various fillings and sauces. Because Mexican food is currently so popular, they are available in most supermarkets.

Mexican Pizza

Serves 2

Garnish this Mexican-style "pizza" with shredded lettuce and serve with salsa or taco sauce.

½ pound lean ground beef
¼ cup chopped onion
¼ teaspoon chili powder
¼ teaspoon cayenne pepper
⅛ teaspoon dried oregano
⅛ teaspoon ground cumin
1 clove finely chopped garlic
¼ teaspoon salt
¼ cup chopped tomato
10-inch flour tortilla
¼ cup chopped green pepper
¼ cup grated Monterey jack cheese
¼ cup grated cheddar cheese

Combine the beef and the onion in a microwavable dish. Cover and microwave on High for 2 to 3 minutes, stirring after 1 minute, until the meat is no longer pink. Drain the meat and return it to the dish.

Stir in the chili powder, cayenne, oregano, cumin, garlic and salt. Microwave on Medium (50 percent) for 2 to 3 minutes. Stir in the tomato.

Preheat an 11½-by-12-inch microwave browning dish on High (100 percent) for 5 minutes.

Spread the meat mixture on the tortilla. Top with the green pepper and both cheeses. Transfer the pizza carefully to the browning dish. Microwave on High (100 percent) for 2 to 3 minutes, until the cheese is melted and bubbly.

Quiche Lorraine

Serves 6 to 8

The classic quiche and oh-so-good! Bake the pie shell first in a conventional oven, but use a microwavable pie plate.

4 slices bacon
1 cup half-and-half
4 large eggs, lightly beaten
⅛ teaspoon ground pepper
⅛ teaspoon ground nutmeg
1 cup (4 ounces) grated Swiss cheese
1 tablespoon chopped scallion
9-inch baked pie shell
¼ teaspoon paprika

Place the bacon on a double thickness of paper towel on a microwavable rack and cover with a paper towel. Microwave on High (100 percent) for 3 to 5 minutes until crisp and browned. Drain the bacon and, when cool, crumble it.

Combine the half-and-half with the eggs, pepper and nutmeg in a 4-cup microwavable measure. Microwave on High (100 percent) for 2 to 3 minutes, just until hot.

Sprinkle the grated cheese, scallions and crumbled bacon on the bottom of the pie shell. Pour the hot egg mixture over the top and sprinkle with paprika.

Set the pie in the microwave on an inverted microwavable saucer and microwave on High (100 percent) for 6 to 10 minutes, until a knife inserted in the center comes out clean. Let the quiche stand for 5 minutes before serving.

When transferring a store-bought frozen pie shell to a microwavable dish, be sure to let the pastry sit at room temperature for 10 to 15 minutes first. A fully frozen pastry shell is brittle and breaks easily when handled.

Shepherd's Pie

Serves 4

As the name suggests, this potato-topped pie was traditionally made for shepherds to take with them when they went up to the hillsides to tend their flocks. A hearty dish made with leftover mashed potatoes, this should certainly satisfy the hunger of your own flock.

4 tablespoons (2 ounces) butter
⅔ cup finely chopped onion
1 medium-size green pepper, chopped
1 cup beef broth
1 pound chopped cooked beef or lamb
3 tablespoons chopped parsley
½ teaspoon dried thyme
Salt and pepper
3 cups mashed potatoes

Place 2 tablespoons of butter in a 2-quart microwavable casserole and microwave on High (100 percent) for 30 to 45 seconds, until melted. Add the onion and green pepper and microwave on High (100 percent) for 3 to 6 minutes, until the vegetables are softened.

Add the broth, meat, parsley and thyme to the casserole. Season with salt and pepper to taste. Cover and microwave on High (100 percent) for 6 to 8 minutes, until the liquid is boiling, stirring once halfway through cooking time.

Put the remaining 2 tablespoons of butter in a microwavable measure. Microwave on High (100 percent) for 30 to 45 seconds or until melted.

Spread the mashed potatoes over the meat and drizzle the melted butter over the top. Cover with wax paper and microwave on Medium (50 percent) for 12 to 16 minutes, until heated through.

INDEX